Whispers of Wisdom

Your Pet Has All The Answers

By: Jamie Lee
© 2017

Forward

This book is a collection of stories about the animals that have shared my life and the lessons they taught me. The stories follow no particular order, so you can read any chapter that calls to you. I believe that if you close your eyes and open the book, you'll be guided to the lesson that's right for you.

Animals have a way of knowing what we need. They certainly have been able to see what I needed to learn, even when I couldn't. My life has been blessed by many different animal beings – cats, dogs, bunnies, birds, frogs, sheep, rodents, and the wildlife in the forest. They all carried with them an important life lesson. They helped me grow into a better person and they guided me to the path I'm on today.

Because of these teachers, I've dedicated my life to translating the language of animals and helping people transform their lives with animal wisdom. I hope that as you read this book, you become aware of the animal teachers in your life; that you honor their wisdom, learn their language, and allow your life to be transformed. The journal that accompanies this book can help you get started.

"Until one has loved an animal, a part of one's soul remains unawakened."

- Anatole France

Introduction

We live in a wounded world. People and animals are suffering and there doesn't appear to be an easy solution. We've been taught how to cover up and ignore our pain so that no one sees it. We throw a tapestry of normality over our problems. Depression, fear, loneliness and grief are buried under expensive clothes, fancy homes, and prestigious careers. Still happiness eludes us.

Somewhere in our past, the human species endured a great forgetting. We've lost touch with the fact that we are spiritual beings. We don't need a new car to be happy; we need a purpose, and we need animals as teachers and equals in our life. We need this as much as we need air to breath.

Mary Lou Randour, author of *Animal Grace* wrote, "Spirituality is not merely about personal salvation, but about moral responsibility and obligation. We are but a strand in the web of life, connected to all life forms, but humans spend most of our time focusing on our differences, rather than our interdependence. How can we possibly move toward spiritual wholeness or grasp the idea of all life being interconnected, if we cannot see beyond our own species?"

I learned to see through the eyes of animals when I was a child. They spoke to me, protected me and shared their secrets of how to live in a state of joy and contentment. They traveled along on my journey to adulthood, and today they continue to provide spiritual healing when my soul is wounded.

My Conversation With God

I've heard it said that before you are born, you have a conversation with God about your purpose on earth – what you want to accomplish during your time on the planet. Then God decides the best way to make it happen. I don't know if any of this is true, but if it is, I know how my conversation with God must have sounded.

"God, I want to go to earth and help all life be free of suffering and help people heal their souls. We both know there's healing in herbs and in the oils of plants. And we know there are Doctors and Dentists and Veterinarians. People have already recognized the healing power of horses and how dogs help disabled people to live independently, but "WE" know there's more. And I want to be the one to show people.

Oh yeah, and It would be really cool if I could be in nature and play with animals all the time."

Then it was God's turn to talk, and I think there was a big smile on her face.

"That's good Jamie, and what you want to do is huge. So in order to heal souls and free all life from suffering, we are going to have to have you experience a lot of trauma yourself. You'll have to learn to heal your own soul first, so you know how to teach others.

Let's start before you are even born.

You father will be broken when he's a baby. His mother, your grandmother, will decide that she can no longer handle her pain and suffering and she will choose to drink acid and end her life violently. Her death will carry a great deal of shame and embarrassment for your family. It will cause your

7

grandfather to give up his children and walk away. But I'll make him a bit of an abusive drunk, so it will for the best.

Your father will go to a stern and strict family. He will rebel and be in and out of trouble. He will grow into a man that appears normal on the outside, but on the inside he's shattered. He is a man that cares only for himself. He lies, cheats and even kills to get what he wants, and he never feels remorse.

Of course, if we're going to put you into a family like this, I have to give you something to hang on to from the very beginning. So, your first home will be in the woods and you will have lots of animals around you. They will be your first teachers. When you are very young, you will spend a lot of time being afraid, and hiding in the woods with your animals. But then the day will come when that changes. Your father will get a new job and you will have to leave your home behind. You will move every school year so that you don't develop close friendships. Your community has to be animals and nature, Jamie.

After a few years of this, you'll move back to those woods you love and then we need something really big to happen."

At that point I probably said, "I hope you're kidding?" But I would already know the answer.

"No, I'm not kidding. You need to experience a total loss of all that you hold dear, something that makes you feel small and disconnected from life. That's what it takes to heal souls.

I know, the clouds will burst high in the hills sending a 50-foot wall of water down the canyon to unleash massive destruction on the town you live in. Over 200 people will die that night; all of your animals will die; many buildings will be destroyed including your home, and your precious forest will be ripped from the earth by the force of the water. In the mornings that follow, the smell of death will fill the air, debris will be scattered all around, and the landscape will be barren and unfamiliar. Nothing will ever look the same again.

After that you're going to begin making a lot of bad, self-destructive decisions. I'll leave the details up to you, Jamie, but I'm thinking drugs, emotionally abusive men, maybe some alcoholism. You get the idea. And you will keep making bad decisions until the day comes when the pain and suffering becomes too great to carry, and you decide you don't want to be alive anymore. Then you have a decision to make – come home to me, like your grandmother did, or turn to the animals and ask them to show you how to heal your soul."

The animals taught me how to heal, but more importantly, they taught me how to live. This book is dedicated to the animal healers in my life.

"Animals share with us the privilege of having a soul."

-Pythagoras

Chapter 1

Keep Your Eyes Wide Open

Do animals have souls? The idea of animals as spiritual beings has been discussed and argued since recorded time. After all, you can't see a soul, so how can you really tell for sure if one exists? The best way is to keep your eyes open. We observe the soul through actions, such as compassion, joy, courage, heroism and forgiveness. We see these actions in people and we also see them in the world of animals.

Jane Goodall, famous for her lifetime research on chimpanzees, told how she observed the behavior of chimpanzees. She said she witnessed "kissing, hugging, embracing, patting on the back, swaggering, shaking of fists, throwing rocks, and all these behaviors were done in the same context as we do them."

Animals are beings who enjoy life. They grieve at loss, they enjoy beauty, participate in social networks, and they love, as demonstrated by the elephants in the Samburu Reserve in North Kenya.

A herd of elephants living at the reserve demonstrate love and compassion on a daily basis. One member of the herd, Babyl, is crippled and walks slower than the rest of the herd. She sometimes even has trouble feeding herself. Without the compassion of her fellow herd members, Babyl would not survive the hardships of the Kenyan landscape.

Rangers have witnessed this compassion first hand. The herd will wait for her when she is having a hard time keeping up with them and they often stop to make sure she hasn't fallen too far behind them. The matriarch of the herd has even been seen feeding her.

Why would elephants give so much care to a member that can't help the herd? The obvious answer is that they care about her. They show emotional intelligence and compassion in their actions towards Babyl.

Dr. Marc Bekoff, Ethologist and award winning author, says, "Animals do have emotions that run the gamut from joy to grief to anger." So animals do have emotions and they express them in a raw, unfiltered way. Their joy is contagious and their grief is deep and devastating.

I have witnessed animals expressing compassion and grief many times in my life. One of the most vivid of these memories is when Zooby, my 14-year-old Jack Russell, made her transition. Zooby had been my only dog for 11 years and she liked being the queen of the house. Then a foster dog came to live with us. Zooby wasn't thrilled about having him in our home, but he seemed to understand her top dog position and things were relatively good between them. Zooby's good nature was put to the test when two more fosters were added to the household. She definitely was not thrilled with their addition, and with each one, she would challenge them to a fight, just to let them know who was in charge.

The last foster that came into our life was a 12 year old Chow Chow. She had been neglected most of her life and suffered from severe arthritis. She was in constant pain and she feared people. Fortunately for us, she loved other dogs and had no problem allowing Zooby to continue her reign.

Tulip had only been living with us for five months when Zooby began having trouble walking. A medical examination found that she had an inoperable malignant tumor on her spine. I had to accept that we were in a hospice situation. I was devastated.

Zooby's health declined rapidly. When the day came that she was unable to lift herself up off her dog bed, I made the difficult decision to have her euthanized. The evening before her appointment she was lying on her dog bed under the influence of pain medication. A co-worker stopped by to check on me and came into the room where Zooby was resting. Tulip, the Chow Chow was lying right beside the bed. She looked up cautiously at my friend.

"Is she friendly?" he asked hesitantly, looking at Tulip.

"Oh, yes," I replied. "She wasn't when she first came, but she's getting more comfortable around people everyday."

"Then why does she keep looking at the door?"

It was then that I noticed Tulip would eye my friend cautiously, then look at the door, look back at my friend, and then back to the door. She seemed to be telling him she was on guard and he wasn't needed here.

She got her message across too; my friend left. I still smile when I think how, after living together for a short time, most of that time being bossed around by Zooby, Tulip was by her side, protecting her when she could no longer protect herself. I knew I was looking at a compassionate soul.

I mourned after Zooby made her transition. I remember spending the weekend on the couch, crying. After several days of feeling tired and numb, I finally came alive enough to see the other dogs in the house were mourning too. Tulip wasn't eating much, and Skip, a 12-year-old dachshund that was usually by my side, was sleeping on Zooby's bed in the laundry room. I had moved it into the room to be washed after she died but couldn't find the energy to do household chores or to be present for the other dogs. That was about to change.

The other pups were grieving her loss too, and it was time to provide the leadership they needed. As soon as I embraced my life again, there was joy in the house.

Animals are constantly displaying soulful actions. They have a lot to teach us about compassion, life and death, if we are paying attention. I learned that with Zooby's death. I had gotten lost in my grief and missed the lessons going on around me, but the animals in my home were still teaching me. Animals may live outside of words, but they are always sharing their wisdom with us. And when we learn to master this skill and communicate with animals, our lives can be transformed.

Lesson One

Animals are spiritual beings.

Animals reveal their soul through their actions and their
emotions. They are a strand in the web of life, just as humans
are a strand, and their lives matter no less than ours. They
deserve to be treated as we wish to be treated – with
kindness, love and respect.

"If you have men who will exclude any of God's creatures from the shelter of compassion and pity, you will have men who will deal likewise with their fellow men."

— *Francis of Assisi*

Chapter 2

The Sheep That Loved Cows

When I was five years old, I had the opportunity to help raise a lamb that had been rejected by his mother and to learn about following my soul's calling, even if it goes against the norm.

My uncle owned a very large sheep and cattle ranch, and every spring he had lambs that were rejected by their mothers. It doesn't happen often, but if an ewe can't provide enough milk due to illness or age, she will refuse to nurse. These lambs faced a grim future without their mother to care for them. One year my parents told my sister and me that we were taking a trip to the ranch. I loved going to the ranch to be around all the animals so of course I was excited.

My uncle greeted us when we arrived. "Let's go see the lambs," he said. I could hardly stay in my skin. Babies! I couldn't wait.

When we went out to the barn, there was a tiny, scared lamb off by himself. "He's the one," my uncle said.

"OK," was my father's reply. Then he told me the best news I had ever heard. "We are going to take him home and try to save him. He'll die without his mother. But you girls will have to do all the work – bottle feeding, cleaning the stall and checking the heat lamp he'll need to stay warm."

My sister and I were ecstatic and a bit sad when we found out that my uncle would be bringing him to our house. To a five year old, it seemed perfectly clear that he could have ridden in the back of the car with us, but the adults held a different view. It gave us time to prepare his stall and get bottles and food.

By the time he arrived, we had everything ready. We had made a makeshift barn with boards that leaned against our house. We covered the ground with shavings and hung a heat lamp above his area to keep him warm. It wasn't the typical home for a baby lamb, but it was created with love.

As soon as he arrived, we prepared his first bottle. As we watched him eagerly gulp down his meal, my sister and I began thinking of names. We agreed on Whistlebritches. Now that I'm an adult, I have no idea how we came up with the name, but it was perfect at the time.

I spent the next few months feeding Whistlebritches and watching him grow. He was healthy and happy and he loved being around people. If we left the back door open, as we often did in the summer, he would walk into the house and eat vegetables off the counter. My sister and I would laugh when he ate carrots that had been harvested that morning. Our mother, however, didn't see the humor in it. It certainly wasn't normal sheep behavior.

As he got bigger, I wanted to take him everywhere, so I decided I would try to walk him on a leash. That didn't work out so well, as Whistlebritches preferred to be leash free. My five-year-old pulling power was no match for his stopping power, so I gave up on that idea.

Whistlebritches had been with us for several months and had grown very big, when he began displaying adolescent behavior. He liked to butt things - including people. Unfortunately, he decided to butt my mother while she was preoccupied with hanging clothes out to dry. The next thing I knew, Whistlebritches was going back to the ranch.

I was heartbroken. I missed my friend tremendously, but I took comfort in knowing he was with other sheep and that I could see him again.

Several months later, my family went to visit my uncle. I couldn't stop talking about Whistlebritches and was excited to see him. When we arrived, my uncle took us out to a pasture. All I saw was cattle; I didn't understand. Then my uncle told me to look closer. That's when I saw him. In the middle of the cattle was one lone sheep.

"Whistlebritches?" I asked.

"Yup. I put him out with the other sheep but he wouldn't go near them. He's afraid of other sheep, but he loves cows, so he goes out to graze with the cattle. Darndest thing I've ever seen."

Whistlebritches had a rough start, but I'm not sure he knew it. He just lived in the moment, and he lived the life that was given to him. He enjoyed the company of humans, he was curious, and apparently he preferred the company of cows to his own kind. It wasn't normal sheep behavior, but Whistlebritches didn't care. He was living life on his terms.

Lesson Two

It's Your Life! Live It!

Don't be afraid to follow to your soul's longings and carve your own path. It's the only way to be truly happy. In the moments when I am torn between doing what's expected and doing what my soul urges me to do, I remember Whistlebritches, the little lamb that lived life joyfully on his terms.

"Perhaps the greatest gift an animal has to offer is a permanent reminder of who we really are."

- Nick Trout

Chapter 3

Tough Times Call For A Furry Blanket

Growing up with animals taught me about the power of compassion. I was raised around chickens, rabbits, lambs, dogs, cats and wildlife. I witnessed them showing kindness to each other every day, something I did not see in my human family. It's no surprise that after growing up in an extremely dysfunctional family, I ended up married to an alcoholic.

I was in a bad marriage, I was severely depressed, I was only 28 years old, and I wanted to die. I was sitting on the bed with a gun in my hand, trying to decide if I should kill myself, or kill my husband, or kill both of us, when I experienced a moment of grace. My animals came to my mind. I was sharing my life with two kitties and my dog, Tai Pan. I knew if I died, there would be no one to care for my pets. They would most likely go to the shelter where they stood little chance of getting out alive. Not only would they die, but they would experience a great deal of fear and depression while in the shelter. Their last days would be as painful as mine were. I knew in that moment that we were in this situation together. They deserved to have the best me and I deserved to be my best. I made a decision to get help.

During this time of recovery, my animals were my rock, especially Tai Pan. TaiPan was a strong and determined Chow Chow that watched over me and taught me to take responsibility for my own happiness. We had gotten in the habit of getting up and walking every morning before work. For our two-mile walk together we got up at 4am. Every morning, it didn't matter if it was dark, cold or rainy, we went for our walk together.

On the weekends, I wanted to sleep in, but Tai Pan had other plans. He would jump up on the bed and stand beside me nose to nose. He was watching my eyes, and the moment they opened or even fluttered, he began to bark. It was time for our walk and my think time!

I caught on to what he was doing, so when I sensed him beside me, I would lay perfectly still. "Don't open your eyes. Don't open your eyes," I'd tell myself. It never worked. A 65 lb. Chow Chow intent on going for a walk, standing nose to nose with you, can be a determined force. I would flinch first and open my eyes. That's all it took, and I knew it was time to walk and think.

I'm so grateful that Tai Pan was there for me. If he hadn't been so insistent that I get up and walk, it would have been easy to sink into despair and just pull the covers over my head. But Tai Pan would have none of that. He understood that we are responsible for our own happiness. He knew that when I wanted to quit, he needed to push me harder. I'm so grateful that he did. He helped me out of a dark place and walked with me into the light.

That is the way it is with animals. If we are willing to accept them as our teachers, the possibilities to transform our lives are limitless. If we listen to their wisdom, we can heal and move forward.

Many years later, it was the animals that taught me how to release anger and grief. While attending an animal Reiki teacher workshop, I spent three beautiful days at Bright Haven, the most amazing animal sanctuary, nestled in the wine country of California. There were beautiful old trees and green pastures, surrounded by fields of grapes. It was home to senior and disabled animals.

23

During the teacher training, we learned many new meditations to share with animals. In the afternoon of the last day, everyone in the class was getting tired, and our brains were on overload. We were given the assignment to pick an animal and meditate for 30 minutes. I went out to an area that had been calling to me the entire weekend. I went to see the cows. They were in a field, surrounded by tall, old cottonwood trees.

Shortly after I began the meditation, I noticed the cows were not coming towards me. That was odd because until now they always came into the Reiki energy. Then, in my mind's eye, I saw the image of a buffalo and a gorilla. Suddenly, I felt a great sadness, and I was overcome with grief and anger. I tried to concentrate more, but it wasn't working. I began to cry. I walked across the field to the horses. One very shy and skittish horse came up to me. I tried to offer him Reiki, but I knew I couldn't. I was angry and sad and grieving. All I could feel was the pain that humans have caused the animals of the world. We stood together for a short time; he was offering me comfort while I was lost in anger and pain. Then he walked away, and I felt defeated.

When everyone returned to our class area at the end of the meditation, we went around the room, talking about our experience. I could feel the emotion welling up in me again, but I was determined not to cry. When my turn came to speak, all I could do was cry.

After I was finally able to explain what happened, it was time for our last meditation of the class. By this time, I was ready to be done. I needed time to process what had happened out in that field. Our assignment this time was called the Healing Heart Bridge. This is where you imagine a bridge extending out from your heart and invite the animals to come forward. They may do whatever they want at this point, but they have been invited into your heart.

I was still feeling vulnerable from the last meditation, so I decided to stay inside and work on a cat that was resting in a sunroom. I was tired, but I began the meditation. My first visitor to the bridge was a large male lion.

I remember thinking, "Oh no! I can't do this again."

Then I heard him speak to me. In a firm but kind voice he said, "Come with me now!"

The next thing I knew, a sea of tall grass surrounded me. The grass was so tall, I couldn't see over it. All I saw was the grass and the lion's back, his tail swishing back and forth. I followed him.

After a short time, we came to a clearing in the grass, and I began to get flashes of other animals – wild animals, my current pets that lived with me, pets that had made their transitions. The images came very quickly, and I began to feel a sense of peace. I felt the warmth of the sun on my face, and I felt protected. I wanted to stay there, but it was time to go back. As suddenly as the lion had appeared, he was gone. I knew I received something big from the animals, but I wasn't able to put it into words. That would come a few weeks later when I was home.

I was home and I had been wracking my brain for the lesson but had come up short. I was telling a friend about my experience when I heard myself say it.

"It felt like I was in a hurricane. The pain and grief I felt around the suffering of animals was like the bands of the storm. When the hurricane first makes land, it brings bands of destruction. It's a dangerous place that can take lives and destroy property. Then the eye of the storm comes, and the wind stops, the sun shines, and it feels peaceful."

I realized in that moment that the suffering of animals, all animals, is like a hurricane. If we stay caught in anger and pain, we will soon run out of energy and drown in our grief. But if we move to the eye, a place of peace and stillness, we can affect change. The more I am able to be in that place of stillness, the larger it grows.

Tight Roping Through Life – Here's Your Safety Net

Animals have always been my safety net in life. When I was young, my family moved every school year for my father's job. It was difficult. The stress of the move affected everyone in the family, and as soon as we got comfortable, my sister and I had another move and a new school to face.

I was always nervous, afraid and unsure as I started a new school year. I was the new kid that didn't know anyone, but my animals were always there for me – even if friends were not. Animals gave me the courage to face new, unknown challenges.

An angel in fur protected me even before I consciously turned to animals to help with the stress and fear of unknown schools.

Buckles taught me to feel safe. Growing up in a dysfunctional home, I never felt safe. As a child, I was always afraid, except when I was with Buckles. He was an adult Airedale, and he was my protector and friend. He kept me safe as I was playing in the woods.

Pet people know the comfort animals provide. We know they help quiet the pain of a friend's broken promise. They ease the embarrassment of a poor presentation in the boardroom. They help us forget all the reasons why we can't do something, and help us remember why we can.

Lesson Three

Animals Are Our Safety Net

When we fight the current of life, we struggle. We may suffer depression, anger, anxiety and even death. But when we allow the current of life to carry us forward, we are liberated. Animals teach us how to jump into the current of life. They are asking each and every one of us not to drown in suffering. They need us to rise above it into a place of love, compassion and quiet. Their lives depend on it and so do ours.

"There is no psychiatrist in the world like a puppy licking your face."

-Ben Williams

Chapter 4

When The Underdog Wins

I first met Skip in the parking lot of a veterinarian's office. He had been rescued from a kill shelter in California and transported to Las Vegas with two other dogs that were going into a rescue group's care. He was a 10-year-old dachshund. His coat was dull, and my nose told me he hadn't had a bath in a very long time. His former owners had dumped him at the shelter because he was old and slow and they didn't want him anymore. He was sad and confused and probably wondering where his family went. I took one look and knew I wanted to help him.

I took him home to introduce him to Zooby. If all went well, I would foster him and help him find his forever home. Zooby began non-stop sneezing, so in addition to being uprooted from his home and traveling across the state, Skip was now about to receive a bath his first night.

I set up a pen for him to sleep in the kitchen. I always let my dogs sleep with me, but since he was a foster and would be going to another home, I didn't want to encourage any habits that might prevent him from being adopted.

Skip came with some problems; he was overweight, he wasn't neutered or house trained, and his back leg was weak, probably why he was so slow. We immediately began his rehabilitation. He was neutered. I changed his diet to a healthy food, and I began with short walks around the block. I began to see a physical change in him, but he was still depressed. He would put himself into his pen and just sleep. I wanted him to be happy and just had to find his perfect forever home.

It's not easy to find new homes for senior dogs, especially if they are not perfectly house trained, but I held out hope that the right home would come along. I witnessed Skip losing weight and walking further. As the weeks went by he could go on the complete walk with Zooby. I was so proud of him, and then I began to worry. What if the people that adopt him don't walk him and his leg gets weak again? What if they don't like the fact he isn't housebroken and take him to a shelter? What if? What if? What if?

At the adoption events I took him to, I found myself sitting behind counters and large kennels. I was keeping him out of sight so I could watch the people looking for dogs. I was determined that nothing bad was going to happen to him again.

Skip had been with me a few months when I was preparing to go visit family for Thanksgiving. Skip was in good physical shape but he was still sleeping in the kitchen and he was still sad. I knew I couldn't take a chance on him being hurt again, so I called the rescue up and told them I wanted to adopt him. The adoption was final before I left for the holiday.

Zooby had traveled many times and was the perfect traveling companion, but I wasn't sure about Skip. I needn't have worried – he rode great! To get to my sister's house was a two-day trip, so I had a room reserved half way through the trip. Our first night we checked into the motel and Skip went running around the room and spied a phone book on the lower shelf of the nightstand. It was at his level! He immediately attacked the phone book and began shredding it. I put a stop to his fun, hid the phone book, and the rest of the night was uneventful. I let Skip sleep with us on that trip. After all, he now had a home where he was welcomed in the bed.

Skip displayed perfect manners at my sister's. He got along with her dogs, and there was no shredding of anything. The problem was, he wouldn't come out of our room. I would sit in the living room and coax him out, only to have him appear in the doorway, look around and run back to his kennel. He wasn't sure what was going on, but he had no intention of being left. Maybe I should have told him it was already official; he was home.

A week later, we arrived back home and Skip let me know that he understood we were family. As soon as he entered the house, he ran to the toy box and grabbed a toy. He took off running as fast as he could. He came back without the toy, grabbed another one, and off he went. Skip did this five times, grabbing a toy, running off, and coming back without it. I went to check the other rooms and in the middle of each room was a toy. Skip was marking his territory; he knew he was home.

Skip – the little dog with two inch legs, lived seven more years being adventurous, determined to get what he wanted, and refusing to back down to anyone. He liked belly rubs; he'd steal goodies out of any purse someone foolishly left low to the ground; he was a tenacious hunter of cockroaches, and he made me laugh. This little dog that others had given up on because "he was old and slow and they didn't want him anymore" taught me to never give up, even when the odds are against me.

Another Super Hero

I had been asked by the staff of Little Friends No Kill Animal Shelter to send Reiki to one of the dogs in their care. It was a pit bull named Vegas that needed to be the only dog in the home. He had been with them for a year and was beginning to lick and self-mutilate. They knew he needed to find a home soon, but his emotional issues had to be addressed. It was Reiki to the Rescue!

Shortly after I began, the Director called me up and said he had stopped licking.

"Why would he do that? Do you think it could be the Reiki?"

I was sure of it. From then on I sent Reiki to Vegas on a regular basis. Within a few months I got the best news ever. A woman with no other animals had adopted him and she was a Reiki Master. Vegas could now look forward to spending his days in his own home, on his mom's Reiki table.

When Pigs Fly

When I first met Flip, he didn't like me. In fact, he didn't like many people. Flip was a large, senior farm pig at Windy's Ranch & Rescue. He had trouble walking because his back legs couldn't support his weight anymore. The founder of Windy's asked me to come work with him but because of his temperament, she didn't want anyone close to him.

I would offer Reiki to Flip from a distance and I let him choose to accept it or not. In the beginning, he spent most of his time in his house, trying to ignore me, but during his sessions I would hear him grunting. Then I began to notice him coming out and moving around more. He would be out in the pasture or in the straw with the other pigs. He still moved slowly but he was out being sociable.

On one of my visits there was a large group that had come for a tour and, to my surprise, Flip was out. The people on the tour had lined up for a picture and they were holding carrots. Flip was walking down the line, taking a carrot from each one of them. The visitors loved it and apparently so did Flip. When the last carrot was gone, Flip found a nice shady spot to lie down. He was flashing the biggest smile I had ever seen. The pig that hated people was looking perfectly content to have visitors.

Lesson Four

Never stop believing in yourself.

We create our life with our intentions. What we think about comes about. So that means what we read, what we watch on TV, what we think about, it all matters. Never allow others to plant a seed of doubt, and never stop believing in yourself.

"Each and every animal on earth
has as much right to be here as
you and me."

-Anthony Douglas Williams

Chapter 5

The Dog Everyone Gave Up On

Tulip was taken to the shelter at 8 years old. I first saw her picture on my rescue feed two years later and she stole my heart. She was a blue Chow Chow that was in need of a home. After having raised Tai Pan from a puppy, I had developed an appreciation for the breed. At the time, I already had three dogs and I lived in a very small house. I couldn't even foster her.

Two more years passed and I had just moved into a home of my own. It had everything I was looking for: one level, no HOA, and a large lot. I was in the process of planting and preparing my lot for the pups when I took a break to check email. There she was – Blue (as she was known then) - looking for a home.

"How can that be? I thought. I first saw her two years ago. I immediately called the rescue that posted her.

I found out that she had a very sad story. She had apparently been a backyard dog that was taken to the shelter with her brother. Both dogs shared a kennel and they were aggressive towards the workers. Her brother died, and she became depressed and stopped eating. The workers were afraid that Tulip was going to die so they began to put other dogs in her kennel.

It seemed to work and pull Tulip out of her depression. Unfortunately, her kennel mates were often adopted, leaving her alone once again. Tulip spent several years going through the loss of those she loved. The rescue assured me she was good with dogs; it was people she could take or leave. But they felt that, if I let her get to know me on her timeframe, things would work out.

I understood the breed so I wanted to try.

Tulip made her trip to the vet before coming to my home. At that time, she needed 7 teeth removed because her mouth was infected, she was suffering from a severe skin infection brought on by her unkempt coat, and she had arthritis in every vertebra of her spine.

She arrived at my home, shaved to the skin and taking antibiotics and Rimadyl for pain.

The rescuer that picked her up from the vet's brought her into my garage. She told me that that Tulip had slipped away from her while leaving the vet's office, making a break for freedom, and she had to chase her down a busy street. "She may be old and have arthritis, but she can run when she wants to!" she said.

We closed the garage door and slipped the lead off of her. Tulip made a dash out the dog door and into the yard. It was secure so I let her settle in. When night came, I tried to get Tulip in the house, but she was having none of it. She just backed away so I let her stay outside.

That's how it went for the next two weeks. She refused to come inside or even come near me. I would take her food dish outside, sit a distance away, and wait for her to come eat. I kept moving closer to the food dish and she would cautiously eat, being sure to always keep an eye on me.

Tulip showed no signs of aggression – just fear. This poor dog was terrified. I called my friend, a professional dog behaviorist, for help. We spent a full day working with her before we were finally able to put a lead on her and bring her inside. After that day, I saw Tulip's spirit bloom.

She became a protector and grandmother figure to the little dogs. They would playfully jump on her, crowd in on her bed so they could be next to her, and one of them had an obsession with Tulip's mouth. She would keep pawing at her mouth until Tulip opened it and let her look inside.

Tulip spent her days patrolling the garden, and going from one side of the house to the other. She lay on her bed in the house, strategically located so that she could see the front and back door. She went from running from people to demanding attention.

To celebrate her transformation, I hosted a Coming Out Party for Tulip and invited all the people that knew her as Blue. I wanted them to know that their efforts with her were not in vain, and to see her as the loving dog she really was. I didn't check with Tulip on the party, but I guess I should have. She was not up to receiving company that day and appeared disgusted as people arrived. She would come to the door and then do her famous wiggle to the bedroom.

The only time the party girl came out of the bedroom was when one of the guests got the little dogs excited. My friend and vet, along with her assistant, both knew Tulip and witnessed her transformation and they came to the party together. Her assistant, Barb, got down on the floor and was playing with the other pups, pounding on the floor and getting them excited. They were running around and barking and having a blast when Tulip trotted out of the bedroom and came nose to nose with Barb, not in an aggressive way, but more like, "what do you think you're doing stirring up those little dogs?" Barb immediately jumped back on the couch. "Sorry Tulip", she said.   With that, Tulip gave a snort of disgust and headed back to the bedroom. Everyone laughed, including Barb.

For the next four years I watched Tulip transform into a gentle, affectionate animal being. She loved people, attention, her yard, and her pack. Not only were the changes evident in her, she changed me too. I went from believing that love can transform anything to knowing it can.

Lesson Five

Love and compassion transform everything.

There are only two choices we must make in life – to look at everything through the eyes of love or to look through the eyes of fear. Fear keeps us trapped in the darkness. It breeds anger, hate and unhappiness. But miracles happen when we look at everything with love.

"We can judge the heart of a man by his treatment of animals."

-Immanuel Kant

Chapter 6

The Body Guards On Duty

Humans and animals have been intertwined since the beginning of time. Animals have often aided us in our growth and survival. If we open our minds to the possibility, we can see how animals have worked to keep us safe from harm. We see this in our pets, but we can also see it in animals in the wild.

In the book, *The Emotional Lives of Animals*, Marc Bekoff describes multiple instances where animals go out of their way to protect humans.

In Ethiopia, three lions rescued a young girl that had been kidnapped by a gang of men, looking to sell her into a life of slavery. The girl was crying when suddenly the lions appeared. They surrounded the child, keeping her safe. The gang ran off, but the lions stayed until the rangers found the girl. According to Sergeant Wondimu Wedajo, "They stood guard until we found her and then they just left her like a gift and went back into the forest." (*The Emotional Lives of Animals,* Marc Bekoff)

In New Zealand, many people witnessed the protective nature of animals. A group of people was swimming in the ocean, when suddenly a pod of dolphins appeared and began to circle protectively around the swimmers. The dolphins began to push the swimmers closer and closer together. Later the swimmers learned that there was a great white shark in the area. The dolphins were protecting the swimmers. (*The Emotional Lives of Animals*, Marc Bekoff)

I have also witnessed this protective nature with my own animals. I remember the first time I noticed my Jack Russell terrier's ability to protect. Zooby was young, wild, and full of energy when we went over to my friend's house for supper. Wanda was raising her two young children by herself after her husband left them. When her daughter, Morgan, was seven, she began having seizures. Wanda definitely had her hands full, and the four of us acted as a family.

After the children had gone to bed for the night, it was our quiet time to talk. Wanda and I were chatting about our life when suddenly Zooby ran back to the bedroom. I knew she was going to jump on the kids and wake them up, so we both jumped up and ran to stop her. But Zooby hadn't been waking up the children. She had been protecting them and alerting us to a problem. We discovered that Morgan was having a seizure. From that day on, I never doubted Zooby's desire to protect.

Pets Are Good For Us

Anyone that has loved and shared their life with an animal knows – PETS ARE GOOD FOR US! The people that haven't had their souls open to the love of an animal don't understand those of us who have. That's very sad. Not only are they missing out, but the animals also miss out on getting the respect they deserve.

For many years, science put animals into a category of soulless, thoughtless creatures which were only capable of following instincts. UGH! Science got that all wrong and, thankfully, they are beginning to come around. Check out some of the "facts" that research has uncovered. (We knew this all along!)

- Stroking or petting an animal has been shown to decrease blood pressure and/or heart rate for the person. (Eddy 1996, Sorek & Terke, 2003)

- Stroking or petting an animal has been show to decrease blood pressure and/or heart rate for the pet too! (McGreevy, Righetti & Thomson, 2005)

- Presence of a dog in a nursing home resulted in happier, more alert and more responsive residents. (Salmon & Salmon, 1982)

- Pet owners are significantly more likely to still be alive one year after a heart attack than non-pet owners. (Erika, Friedman, Katcher, Lynch, 1980)

Lesson 6

Angels in Fur, Feathers or Scales

Animals are watching over us – protecting us and guiding us to a life of happiness. They protect our homes, our bodies and our spirits. They are the exact medicine for what ails people and they are a lot more fun than popping a pill.

Chapter 7

How Much Is The Kitten in the Clothes Pin Bag?

When I was seven, my family was beginning a road trip across several states to visit my mother's family. For some reason, we needed to stop at the ACE hardware store on the way out of town. I was very familiar with the store and the manager, Mr. Evans, since I often accompanied my parents on shopping trips. My father went inside, and while we were waiting for him to return, I saw a small, yellow kitten hiding between the garbage cans that were on display outside the store.

Of course I had to go meet him. So, I hopped out of the car and walked up to the kitten. He didn't run or hide, instead he came out and rubbed against my leg. I was instantly in love. I had to have this kitten. My seven-year-old mind figured that if he was at the hardware store, he must be for sale. But first, I would have to run it by my parents.

I have spoken about my childhood already in this book. It was a cold, dysfunctional and frightening place. But one thing that was true, when it came to animals, my parents almost always said yes to me.

I gathered up my courage and showed them the kitten.

"Can we afford him?" I asked.

My parents looked puzzled, so I continued.

"He must need a home, or he wouldn't be for sale at the store."

Then my mother spoke.

"They don't sell kittens here. Go ask Mr. Evans if he belongs to anyone."

Panic set in. Speaking to an adult was a terrifying for me. I was a very shy child and I would hide from people I didn't know, but not this day. I mustered up every ounce of courage I could find and walked into the store.

"Excuse me Mr. Evans, does the little kitty outside belong to anyone?" The fear of speaking to an adult was overwhelming.

"That little thing? No, he's been hanging around for a couple of days and I think he's a stray. If you want him you can take him."

I was ecstatic and ran out of the store, slipping on my way out, but I didn't care. I felt like I had slayed a dragon by facing my fear. And I had a new kitten!

Now remember, we were on our way across several states to visit family. Anyone that has ever lived with a cat probably doesn't put traveling cross-country with a cat at the top of their "things to do list," but we did. The next thing I knew, my mother was coming out of the store with a kitty box, dishes and some food.

As I look back on the situation, I think my parents said yes to this kitty because every time we visited my mother's family, my cousin would try to give me an animal to take home. There were always tears when it came time to leave and I was told we couldn't spend two days in the car with a kid goat or a bunny or a puppy. The tearful goodbyes would be avoided with this tiny kitten.

I named the kitten R.C., and he turned out to be the perfect kitten. He rode well, used his litter box, and he didn't cry at all. It was almost as if he had been waiting for me that day. After two days on the road, we arrived at my grandparents'. My grandmother believed that animals belonged outside and wouldn't let RC in the house. Fortunately, they had a screened-in porch that he was allowed to stay in. Every night, RC would climb into my grandmother's clothespin bag that was hanging on the porch and go to sleep. In the morning, he would slap at me to help him down. I looked forward to our morning routine.

RC stayed on the porch and never even tried to run off while we were there. When it came time to go home, he was the perfect travel companion once again.

RC traveled with us for several years as we moved around for my father's employment. He wasn't afraid of the car. He wasn't afraid of new surroundings. He didn't seem to get upset about anything. Any cat owner will tell you this is very unusual behavior for a cat. But RC just took everything in stride. He was the tiny little kitten that taught me a big lesson - live in the moment and go with the flow.

Lesson Seven

Go With The Flow

We accomplish more when we stop trying to force things. Life becomes joyful and easy when we live in the moment. This is where all are dreams come true – in the flow of life.

"An animal's eyes have the power
to speak a great language."

-Martin Buber

Chapter 8

Are You Smarter Than The Average Pet?

HOW MANY DOGS DO YOU SEE?

?

ANSWER 19

A good friend of mine was fostering an 8-year-old bulldog mix named Mocha, She had been surrendered because of a food allergy. She was brindle colored, about knee high and, from the rear, she looked like a baby hippo. She was adorable. I saw her picture and fell in love, and so did my friend. She agreed to foster.

At the time, I was fostering a dog from the same rescue and I would see my friend and Mocha at the adoption events. With each event, Mocha would become more and more aggressive towards the other dogs. At the end of the event, my friend would load her up in the car, drive home, and watch her lounge peacefully with the other dogs in the household.

No matter what my friend tried, Mocha's behavior continued. No one was interested in an aggressive dog, so Mocha always came home with my friend. One day we were talking and my friend was telling me how worried she was about finding Mocha a home.

"I don't know what to do with Mocha. She's a great dog and she behaves at my house, but let me take her to an adoption event and she turns mean. She'll never get adopted if she keeps this up."

"I don't know what you're talking about. It appears she already has a home," I said.

"I can't adopt her. I want to help a lot of dogs and, if I adopt her, I can't take any more dogs into my home. There's just no room. I couldn't foster any more."

My friend was sure the best thing to do was to find Mocha a home and foster another dog.

Mocha had other ideas.

It took awhile, but Mocha was finally able to break down my friend's wall and make her realize that she already had the perfect home. Yes, she adopted her, and Mocha never showed aggression again.

Queen Of The House

Pets really can outsmart us. I found that to be true when I adopted my Jack Russell puppy, Zooby. I named her for her exuberance, and if I had any questions about how smart animals really are, Zooby was about to answer them.

I lived in a mobile home with a counter dividing the kitchen and living room. I puppy-proofed the house, picked up things that would be attractive to a puppy, and moved the cat dish to the counter to keep Zooby out of his food.

One day my cat, DC, jumped on the couch and onto the counter to eat. I walked to the back of the house to get something, and when I came back, there was Zooby, standing in the kitchen sink. She had seen DC use the couch to get on the counter and thought it would be great fun. That day I registered for an obedience class and rearranged the furniture.

Zooby displayed her teaching skills all the time, but I remember the day she schooled me in Animal Reiki. I had just completed my first Level I Reiki class and I was excited to try it out. I was sitting on the couch with Zooby by my side, resting. Since she didn't slow down very often, I thought this would be a perfect opportunity to give her Reiki. I had so much to learn! The minute my hands touched her, she jerked her head up and glared at me. She was not happy and she jumped off the couch, went across the room and lay down.

From that moment on I was never able to offer her Reiki through touch. Of course, now I realize that I did everything wrong. I didn't ask permission, I didn't set an intention, and I immediately put my hands on her, even though she didn't ask me to. Yes, I had a lot to learn, but this girl was up for the job.

Zooby was constantly challenging my intelligence but she was also offering a great lesson. Her inquisitive nature and her zest for life were contagious. Together we walked, trained and traveled around the country, enjoying and living fully in every moment. She always reminded me that life is good!

Lesson Eight

Animals Are Our Teachers

Animals come to us with lessons to share. They know what we need and they will do everything in their power to help guide us. We may be amused, frustrated, angry or hurt, but we will learn.

"*He who feeds a hungry animal*
feeds his own soul."

-Charlie Chaplin

Chapter 9

When Apes Speak, It's Best To Listen

I was visiting the San Diego Zoo when I was given the opportunity to fine-tune my communication skills with animals.

It was the weekend and the zoo was packed with people. I'm not a big fan of zoos - I would rather see animals living in sanctuaries than being entertainment for people - but I was traveling with a group of people that wanted to go. I figured I could at least offer Reiki to the animals.

We had been walking around for some time when I came to the gorilla enclosure. This enclosure was large. There were big trees and grasses and tires, and it looked like it would be appealing to gorillas. There was fencing around the area and a glass wall where people could stand and watch the gorillas.

On this day, every disrespectful person happened to be standing by the glass. I watched as people taunted the gorillas. They laughed, they made ape noises and pounded on the glass. I was immediately sad and embarrassed to be a member of the human species.

I remember thinking, "What can I do?" The only thing I could do was offer Reiki, so I put my hands down by my side, took a deep breath and began. At that moment, I glanced up and made eye contact with the Silverback. He was far back in the enclosure watching over everything.

I immediately broke the eye contact and looked down, but it was too late. He was up and moving my way. I began to panic. What have I done? Don't come over here. But he kept coming and the crowd became louder and more demonstrative the closer he got.

The old silverback ignored the jeering of the others and came directly up to the glass in front of me. Then he turned around and leaned against the wall, his back directly in front of me.

At the time, I humanized his behavior. I felt like I had insulted him and he was letting me know by turning his back to me. I quickly left. It wasn't until a couple of years later, in an animal communication class, that I was offered another view of our interaction. After telling the story to the group and explaining how bad I felt that day and still felt, the teacher offered her thoughts.

"You know, if an ape is upset with you, he's going to be very clear about it. He would have pounded on the glass or thrown poop at you. By coming up to you directly and turning his back, he was just acting like a silverback would with any member of his group. How lucky you were to have him as a Reiki teacher."

In the two years since my visit, I had never considered that he might have been saying something else to me. I was busy humanizing his behavior. Now I realize what an honor it was for him to come up to me and I wish I would have spent more time with him. It's easy to misread the wisdom of animals.

Lesson Nine

The wisdom of animals is whispered.

We find the secrets to living a vibrant life in the quiet connection we share with animals. Their wisdom is whispered, so we must be willing to become still and listen. It may be difficult at first because there are so many distractions in the world today, but with practice it becomes easier. We learn to listen to their whispers and liberate ourselves from emotional and physical pain.

"Some people talk to animals. Not many listen though. That's the problem."

-A.A. Milne, Winnie-the-Pooh

Chapter 10

Mirror, Mirror On The Wall, Why Are You Covered In Fur

I've heard it said that your vibe attracts your tribe, meaning whatever energy you put out comes back to you. Animals understand this, and they have many ways to teach humans about the true essence of life. Sometimes their behavior mirrors that of their human, and sometimes they behave in the exact opposite way. For example, if the person is high strung, the dog may also be high strung. Or the animal may become ill, forcing the person to slow down to care for them. That's known as modeling.

Why do animals mirror our behavior? I believe it is to get our attention. I don't know of anyone who wakes up in the morning feeling happy and content and thinks to themselves, "My life is great. I better change it." No, usually it takes pain to get our attention, to make us want to change. Animals know this, and by creating strong emotions in us, they encourage us to make the changes we need to make in order to live a life of excellence. (*Animal Lessons*)

I always knew that animals often reflect our behavior, but I was still focused on doing energy work just with animals until one day at Little Friends Animal Shelter. I had spent the day offering Reiki to the animals at Little Friends and was just getting ready to leave when the manager, Karen, came up to me.

"My friend is here with her dog and she's really upset. Her dog has cancer and he's having surgery tomorrow. Would you mind giving him Reiki?"

"Of course," I replied.

I asked her to bring her friend and the dog into the large enclosed outdoor area. The dog immediately began to run around the area without stopping, and the woman immediately began talking. She was telling me that he had cancer and that she was afraid he would die and that he was her first dog and she's never been through anything like this and she didn't think she could do it.

I knew I wasn't going to be able to help anyone the way things were going. I couldn't get the dogs attention, and I couldn't get her to stop talking. Finally, out of desperation, I asked her if I could work on her. She looked a little puzzled, but she agreed.

A chair was brought in and I began to work on her. Within thirty seconds of beginning the session, her dog stopped running frantically around the enclosure, lay at her feet, and began accepting Reiki.

He was mirroring what was going on with his owner. I knew they were feeding off each other, but I did not think by working with her, I would reach him. Now I understand that animals are always teaching and often telling me more about their owner than they are about themselves.

Today, I always begin my work by addressing the relationship and trust that the animal will show me what I need to know.

Another Teaching

A friend of mine also discovered how animals teach us. He and his wife were having trouble with their teenage daughter. Nothing serious, just a teenager testing her limits and disobeying her parents, but it was enough to cause a great deal of stress in the household.

My friend and his wife found themselves arguing over the best way to handle her behavior. They were both frustrated and after a couple of months, their frustration level was at an all time high. Then they noticed something off with their dog, Kelly. She was limping.

They checked her paws but could find nothing wrong. There were no signs that she had hurt herself but the limping continued. They took her to the vet and she, too, found nothing wrong with her. My friend took his dog home and became more aware of her behavior, thinking that maybe he missed something.

He kept a close eye on her but did not discover what might be causing her pain. He was so intent on watching Kelly that he hadn't noticed things with his daughter were getting better. She wasn't acting out any more and his wife wasn't frustrated. He couldn't even remember the last time they fought.

Then, another amazing thing happened. As mysteriously as the limp started, it disappeared. Kelly had been reacting to the fighting and stress level in the house. By getting my friend's attention off the problem, she had given it space to correct itself. Kelly was teaching and guiding her family.

Lesson Ten

Animals are Mirrors

Animals often reflect back the energy of their environment. If your pet is displaying a behavior problem, take a look at what is going on in your life. What is your pet trying to teach you with their behavior?

"The assumption that animals are without rights and the illusion that our treatment of the them has no moral significance is positively outrageous example of Western crudity and barbarity. Universal compassion is the only guarantee of morality."

-Arthur Schopenhauer, *The Basis of Morality*

Chapter 11

How To Survive the Hardest Goodbye

Animal lovers understand the pain of loss, especially if they share their lives with pets. These magnificent creatures come into our lives, steal our heart and often our beds, and bring joy - and eventually great sorrow - into our life. We accept these conditions because the joy that comes from being with them is worth the pain when we must say good-bye.

Losing a pet is something all pet owners fear. They ask themselves, "What will I do when they are gone? How will I get through it?" And then they try very hard not to think about it. The death of a beloved pet is devastating, however we can find some relief when we turn to science.

Quantum Physics teaches us that everything is energy and energy cannot be destroyed. Scientific studies have shown that, if you divide a particle and separate the two parts, they are still connected by an invisible wave of energy.

Scientists did just this. They split a particle, separated them by a large distance and then did something to one of the particles to cause it to react. What they found is that at the same time the first particle reacted, the second particle also reacted. This led researchers to believe that they were still connected.

There is a divine consciousness that connects all life. The problem we face is that we've been taught that we are all individuals and must achieve on our own. We believe that we are separate. Animals know that we are all connected and part of this unified consciousness. They taught me about the connection.

In her book, *Animal Grace*, Mary Lou Randour wrote: "There is no exact moment which we no longer exist. Death is a transition to another state, and if we are sensitive enough, we can participate in the transition."

I always understood this in my mind, but it wasn't until Tulip made her transition that I understood it with my heart.

A cancerous tumor had been found on the back of Tulip's tongue during a routine exam. My vet removed as much of the tumor as she could, but to get everything would require the removal of her tongue, which she did not recommend. I refused to put her through such an extreme surgery and for a year she was on a cancer fighting, Chinese medicine protocol.

A year later, Tulip was still happy and energetic, and then she began throwing up. I consulted with my vet who agreed the cancer had spread. I made it clear that she had been through enough in her 16 years and I wanted her last days to be peaceful.

Tulip's health rapidly declined. I knew it was almost time to say good-bye so I called my vet and made the arrangements for later in the week. I had to report for jury duty the next morning. I thought Tulip would be comfortable until her appointment, but I was wrong. The next morning Tulip seemed disoriented. I hand fed her some meat, but it didn't stay down. I could tell she was beginning her transition and I became angry that I had to report to the courthouse. I called my friend and asked her to come over until I could get back.

I returned home to find Tulip resting on her bed. My friend had cleaned up several messes throughout the day and I was very grateful that Tulip had not been alone. I knew I would have to say goodbye the next morning.

I lay beside Tulip, petting her and letting her know it was okay to leave. I thanked her for all the gifts she had given me. I didn't know she had one more gift before she left.

Tulip became very restless and wanted to go outside. She could not get up without assistance, so I would lift her up and take her outside. She would lie on the grass for a while but then the restlessness came back and she tried to get up. I carried her in and out of the house several times throughout the night. Finally, I placed her on her bed and curled up next to her. I began my Reiki breathing and soon, she was calm. Our breathing became synchronized. It was almost as if I was breathing for her, giving her the energy she needed to make her transition.

We laid together for hours, breathing. I felt our connectedness in my soul. I knew she would always be with me, because we were one.

The vet arrived that morning to assist Tulip in her transition. My other dogs were lying by Tulip's side and two of my friends were there to say goodbye. We spoke of our memories of Tulip and the love we shared for her.

I wanted to anoint Tulip with Frankincense, so I got up from where I was sitting on the floor. I had been in that position for hours, but my legs were not even stiff. I felt like I too had been in a place of transformation instead of the physical world. The moment I dropped the Frankincense oil on her head, Tulip let out a big sign. She was ready to go. We said our good-byes and the Doctor gave her the final injection. Immediately, my parakeet began to sing a beautiful song. I knew her soul was free.

Through a Pet's Eyes

Grief isn't exclusive to the loss of a pet. Animals also experience the pain of loss when they lose a human companion. I learned that from Snow, my mother's Westie.

Snow was her constant companion, so much so that my mother's friends all came to visit at her house because they knew my mom wouldn't leave Snow home alone. He gained the nickname, "The President," from her friends.

Snow and my mother had been together for several years when we received the diagnosis everyone dreads. My mother was beginning her decline into Alzheimer's. After three years it became apparent that my family could no longer care for her and keep her safe, so she was moved to a special nursing facility. Snow lived with my sister and would visit mom on the weekends. It didn't take him long to get into the routine. Every weekend he was by the door, wagging his tail and waiting to go.

Once he was at the facility, Snow went to work greeting all the residents. He would stop by each door and wait for them to greet him before moving on. Eventually he made his way to my mother's room, but not before spreading his own brand of medicine to the other residents. Snow loved the attention, and the people in the facility loved him, too.

One day a call came in from home supervisor. My mother had a stroke and was on the way to the Emergency Room. My sister made it to the hospital in time to say goodbye and watch my mother make a peaceful transition.

When my sister returned home, she called for Snow, but he didn't appear. She started looking. My mother had lived with my sister for a couple of years before her disease required 24 hour care, so Snow had his favorite places. Finally she found him, under my mother's bed, whimpering. He already knew his favorite human had passed, and he never asked to go visit the nursing facility again.

It's not just our pets that grieve. There are many documented cases of wild animals displaying grief. People have reported dolphins struggling to save a dead calf. Gorillas hold wakes for their dead and elephants display grief when a friend or family member dies. Marc Bekoff wrote in "Yes" magazine about a magpie funeral.

"I once happened upon what seemed to be a magpie funeral service. A car had hit a magpie. Four of his flock mates stood around him silently and pecked gently at his body. One, then another, flew off and brought back pine needles and twigs and laid them by his body. They all stood vigil for a time, nodded their heads, and flew off."

Through A Child's Eyes

As a child, I had all kinds of pets, including fish. Unfortunately, they didn't live long because, when I was a child, many people were not aware of the care they needed. I was always heartbroken when one of my pet goldfish died, and I would take it out to a special place in the forest and bury it. There was a ceremony and a child's cross made of popsicle sticks marked the grave. When wild animals began to dig up the area, I made plaster of Paris grave covers to keep them out. I put a small garden fence around my little cemetery to keep animals out, although looking back, I realize it would stop nothing. But I did all these things anyway, because even as a child, it was my way of showing respect for the lives of animals. Today, if I drive past an animal that has been hit and killed on the highway, I blow a kiss to the heavens. It is my way of respecting all life on this place. By honoring all life forms, I've learned that I am a strand in this magnificent web of life. My actions affect all other life forms, a responsibility I strive to honor.

Lesson Eleven

Love is love. It hurts when anyone (human or animal) we love dies, and all life deserves to be treated with honor. It is not only okay to grieve, it is necessary for the healing process. It helps to keep in mind that all life is energy, and energy is never destroyed, it only changes forms. Our loved ones have not left us; they just transitioned to another form.

"If a dog will not come to you after having looked you in the face, you should go home and examine your conscience."
-Woodrow Wilson

Chapter 12

The Miracle Dog

Normally when working with an animal client, I see a gradual change in the issue the animal is suffering from, whether physical or emotional. It takes time for the animal to release the blocks that are stopping them from trusting me. I always tell the pet parent to be patient and not expect burning bush miracles, but rather gradual miracles that happen over time. Once in a while, however, an animal comes into your life to get your attention. That's what happened to me with Gemma.

Gemma was a smaller dog, obviously some kind of a mix, maybe dachshund, maybe corgi, it was hard to tell. But no matter what breed she was, she had a beautiful smile and an unstoppable attitude. I heard about her from a volunteer at Hearts Alive Village Las Vegas (HAVLV), a rescue that I work with ofton. Gemma had come into their care after being rescued from the Henderson Animal Shelter.

Gemma's former owners deserted her in the middle of the night leaving her in the drop-off kennel at the shelter. When the shelter workers found her the next morning, they immediately knew why she'd been abandoned. Gemma's back legs did not work. She was paralyzed.

A paralyzed dog would not have much of a chance at any shelter, and everyone knew it, including a shelter volunteer that also worked with HAVLV. Phone calls were made, and Gemma was soon in the custody of this amazing rescue group and on her way for a complete medical checkup.

Other than her back legs being paralyzed, Gemma's check up was good, and so were her spirits. She spent her days at the Hearts Alive Pet Store with her foster mom, Kelly, scooting around the floor and playing with anyone that was up for a rousing game of chase. Her back legs may not have worked like other dogs, but she didn't let it slow her down.

At night, she went home with her foster mom. Kelly suffered from a debilitating disease that left her in need of a wheelchair and a service dog. Gemma had no problem integrating into the pack, and soon she found herself with her own little doggie wheelchair. Look out! There was no stopping Gemma now. She loved going for walks with her foster mom - Kelly in her electric wheelchair and Gemma with her wheels.

Gemma was receiving great care and lots of love, but my friend still wanted more for her, so she asked if I would send Reiki to Gemma. Of course I said yes. I went to the adoption center to meet Gemma myself, and she was everything my friend said she was: adorable, happy, fast, and totally unaware that she suffered from a disability. I introduced myself to Gemma but the store was busy, so I returned home to offer distant Reiki.

If you are unfamiliar with Reiki, it's important to know that as a practitioner, I am not causing anything to happen. I invite the animal to join me and then I just allow the energy to flow. Energy will always work for the highest good of the animal or person, but they have a voice in the process. It's always up to the animal if they wish to accept the healing energy of Reiki.

There was nothing unusual about the distant Reiki session the night after I met Gemma, but the morning session was a different story. I always feel heat during a session, and that morning the heat I felt was intense. I wasn't aware of anything other than a deep connection with Gemma. When I finished I was famished and needed to refuel. I knew it had been a powerful session, but I wasn't expecting the text I received later that night.

It came from the founder of the rescue – Gemma was walking!

Gemma's recovery was due to love, proper medical care and Reiki. It came at a time when I was questioning if I was really on the right path myself. I had been working hard to help animals with Reiki but it was becoming more difficult to gain acceptance. Shelters were saying 'no thanks' and pet owners didn't understand the benefit of Reiki. I felt like I was on an uphill climb and I was beginning to question my purpose. Then Gemma came into my life and the teacher became the student.

She taught me to trust the energy and its power to heal. She reminded me that the only thing I need to do is to ask for the exact healing that's needed in this exact moment and get out of the way. Gemma brought me the burning bush moment that I needed in my life.

Lesson Twelve

Your Burning Bush Moment

Each and every one of us came to this planet for a reason. We come into life knowing our True Self and our connection to Source, but with time, our memories fade. It is easy to get distracted by life and all that surrounds us in the physical plain. The distractions cause us to forget who we really are and what we came to do. We forget that all life is connected and all life matters equally. Our mission becomes to remove the layers that block our light and remember. If you remain true to your purpose, the Universe will support you. Sometimes we forget this and life becomes hard. Animals are more than happy to act as our 'burning bush moments' and remind us of what we came to do.

Lessons from the Animals at a Glance

Wisdom Whispers

1. Animals Are Spiritual Beings

2. Live Life!

3. Animals Are Our Safety Net

4. Believe in Possibilities

5. Love And Compassion Change Everything

6. Angels Wear Fur, Feathers & Scales

7. Go With The Flow

8. Animals Are Our Teachers

9. The Wisdom Of Animals Is Whispered

10. Animals Are Mirrors

11. Love Is Love

12. Animals Provide Our Burning Bush Moment

Gratitude

This book is the result of a lifetime spent loving and learning from animals. It wouldn't have been possible without the help of my friends and family – human and animal. I'd like to thank those who shared this journey with me. First, a big thank you to the readers for taking time to read this book and for seeking the wisdom contained in the whispers of animals. I'd also like to give a shout out to my editor, Sheryl Green, and my coach, Skye Baloo. Thank you for believing in me and encouraging me on this journey. I'd also like to thank Kathleen Prasad, my Animal Reiki teacher, for blazing the way for all of us that want to serve animals through energy. Last, but certainly not least, I want to thank my friends Judy and Kris for always believing in me. I am truly blessed to have all of you in my life.

www.ingramcontent.com/pod-product-compliance
Lightning Source LLC
Chambersburg PA
CBHW062025040426
42447CB00010B/2146